Welcome to Pursue.

I am so excited that you are embarking on this journey. It is my passion that everyone walks fully connected to the heart of God.

It says in 1 Corinthians 14:1 "Pursue love, and desire spiritual gifts, but especially that you may prophesy." NKJV

Pursue has been written to be a catalyst in your life, to enable you to do exactly as Paul has written.

Be ready to encounter His unrelenting, unconditional love. It is incomprehensible. As you pursue Him, trust He is present and drawing near to you. You are His passion and object of His affection.

One of the greatest gifts and benefits of being a child of God is hearing His voice. For some, this is not new, but we tend to practice 'hearing' Him for others however, we struggle to hear Him, for ourselves. Also, we often lean towards hearing him for what we can do for Him, rather than simple connection. However, this is a "both-and" journey.

The Lord has invited us into a friendship connection. It is about the ebb and flow of doing, out of our connection. This is the starting place of prophetic expression and lifestyle.

Over the next 7 weeks allow Him into spaces of your heart. My prayer is that; you will be renewed and see a relational Father; one who cares about you. I pray that you will experience the depths of His love; live continually in His wrap-around presence and go from glory to glory.

Blessings

Sarah Morgan

Thank you

Thank you to all who helped; Your kindness and grace towards me gave me the courage to keep going.

Gary, thank you for championing this project and believing in me when I didn't. I am so thankful for your love and support.

References and Inspiration:

Mark Verkler: 4 keys to Hearing God's Voice. | Scriptures: All scriptures are New King James Bible. All rights reserved Thomas Nelson since 1978 Copyright 1982 by Thomas Nelson. Used by permission, unless otherwise noted. | Other recourses: Bible Hub and Blue Letter Bible Images: Unsplash

But seek first the kingdom of God and His righteousness, and all these things shall be added to you.

Matthew 6:33

PURPOSE

1

Day 01 /
Intentions.

———

In the beginning God created the heavens and the earth. The earth was without form, and void; and darkness was on the face of the deep. And the Spirit of God was hovering over the face of the waters. Then God said, "Let there be light"; and there was light. And God saw the light, that it was good; and God divided the light from the darkness. God called the light Day, and the darkness He called Night. So the evening and the morning were the first day.

Genesis 1

God created the world with the same intention that He continued to display throughout history. The creation story reveals his relational, redemptive purpose that hasn't changed. His intentions to bring light out of darkness and peace to chaos are revealed from the beginning. His creative nature looks at every situation with one option-to bring life.

Although our shame has produced an automatic response to hide, the Lord is constantly inviting us to bring our full hearts into the light of His love. He wants to bring light and life to the things that we keep hidden. It is not always sin that we are hiding; it can also be the greatness that He has placed within us that we hide out of fear.

Wherever the Spirit of the Lord is, there is freedom. It is His desire today to reveal to you that His intentions are for good and not for evil. It doesn't matter what you are facing, He wants to bring life out of you now. God's demonstration of the great exchange that took place on the cross is the same intention displayed at creation-to give what wasn't deserved.

Reflection

- What other biblical examples can you find, that demonstrate His intention to give in exchange for, or, in the place of something 'dark or missing'?

- What areas in your life has God spoken to you about, that you are still in hiding over?

- Are there promises He has given you, that you haven't quite come to believe yet? Meditate on them and journey with the Lord in changing that.

Day 02 /
His Redemptive Voice.

The voice of the Lord is redemptive in its nature. It's full of love and compassion. It carries wisdom beyond anything natural. No matter what we are facing, He wants to offer life and work everything for the good of those who love Him and are called according to His purpose (Romans 8:28).

Read John 4:1-42
This is one very famous story of how Jesus extends His grace and His redemption towards someone who lived a terrible truth.

We have been taught that the woman at the well didn't deserve social grace because she was a "sinful" woman. We read this out of our own assumptions of what it would mean to have five husbands. However in the cultural context of the times; a woman was only ever allowed to marry again if her husband had died. If they were caught in adultery, she would have been stoned. Even if they had permitted her to remarry after divorce, how many times would she have been allowed?

What if she represented a woman who was cursed. Not sinful as we suppose?

Can you imagine what it would have been like if you had five husbands die on you? How traumatic would that have been? Surely people discussed of how she wasn't one to be around.

"And the one you're now with isn't even your husband". We read that through today's culture lens. However, when you are betrothed, that is the one you are 'with'. Can you just imagine the thoughts that must have been going through this man's head? "If I marry her will I die too?"

Christ came to her and rewrote the Samaritan woman's narrative by coming with the fullness of redemption and compassion. He uses words of knowledge to capture her attention out of her cultural norm.

Either way-if she lead a 'sinful' life or she felt cursed-Christ came to give her new life.

Reflection

- Ask the Lord if there has been a narrative on your life that He would like to redeem?

- What would He like to change in your heart and mind about yourself, your circumstance, or your past?

- Ask the Lord what His thoughts are towards you? Write it down.

As the Father loved Me,
I also have loved you;
abide in My love.

John 15:9

Day 03 /
The Pursuit of Love.

God wants us to encounter His love and salvation. He is so intentional about loving us that He would go to drastic measures just to get our attention.

Read Acts 10
This is a story of how Peter witnesses the supernatural salvation and baptism of the Holy Spirit in a Gentile household. Through multiple visitations from various people, Peter is led to Cornelius' house contrary to his cultural permits.

Through this one scene, we see just how far He will go to change a cultural norm and displace all of the belief systems that were built up over multiple generations. This was true not just for the Jewish people but for the Gentiles also. The Lord's desire for all to be His is dramatically played out through this situation.

The prophetic, hearing God's voice; is there to guide us and lead us just like Christ lead his life on earth. He speaks with His redemptive nature, His consuming and unconditional love. This love has been made available to all who will receive it.

Although the Lord is varied in the way He guides and speaks to us, His primary goal is leading us to be loved by Him and to love others.

Reflection

- Take a moment to record the many ways the Lord speaks uniquely to you.

- Throughout the day, tune into an awareness of His presence, and recognise when He is trying to get your attention; either to show His love for you or someone else. Journal your experience.

- How is the Lord wanting to love you today?

Day 04 /
Faithful Promises.

The Lord is so faithful. From age to age, though the earth may pass away, His word remains the same. His words don't return to Him void. History can prove there's nothing He can't do. He is faithful and true. Though the storms may come and the winds may blow, He remains steadfast. He will be present; ready and able to perform His word.

When the Lord speaks prophetic promise over us, He speaks with the same intention that He did at the beginning. To give light into the darkness, peace to that which is chaos and to bring life where there is death. When we receive prophetic promises we need to understand that He sees things generationally. He is multidimensional; He works in time but also transcends time.

Read Genesis 17 and 18

Though the promise that Abram and Sarai received took time, God was faithful. The promise of being the Father and Mother of nations was like a neon signpost that pointed to what the Lord had planned for their life.

The Lord had other signposts of His faithfulness to remind them of that very promise. Through the day, it was sand; at night, it was the stars. Can you imagine those reminders? There is no way you can get away from sand when you live in a desert! At night, when you look up at the sky, it is hard not to notice the many stars. Every turn Abraham took, he was reminded of what the Lord had promised, even when his circumstances looked the complete opposite.

Proverbs and Psalms consistently speaks of meditating on the promises or His law; to wrap them around our hearts and to "keep them in front of us" (Proverbs 3:3). When we do this we begin to understand that one word can translate over multiple seasons that we go through. He gives us multifaceted words that speak so specifically and uniquely. He causes them to become signposts of His love and faithfulness as we journey through life.

He is so determined to be faithful to that which He has promised. He is always faithful to complete the good work He has started. Let us partner with His prophetic promises, allowing them to build within us trust and confidence that He is good, ultimately leading us into a deeper relationship with Him.

Reflection

- Write down some ways God has shown you He is faithful.

- Is there a specific prophetic promise that you are waiting for fulfilment? If yes: What 'signposts' of His faithfulness has he shown you as a reminder of this promise? Spend some time with Lord in thankfulness and hope of the fulfilment of the promise. If you can't identify any, spend some time with the Lord and ask Him to show you a 'signpost' of His faithfulness.

- Ask the Lord to share His heart for you with regards to the promises and purposes He has for your life.

Day 05 /
A Matter of the Heart.

We have reflected upon the purpose and why of the prophetic. Over the past few days we have discovered the following:

- It is His intention to speak life, light and peace
- His voice is redemptive
- The prophetic leads to salvation and encountering His love
- The prophetic leads us to His faithfulness

Today, we are going to be looking at how it changes the narrative of a person.

Read 1 Samuel 16: 1-13

At times we are so quick to judge others, circumstances and even ourselves. The narrative that we convince ourselves to be true, isn't actually in the heart of God. We hold up a measuring stick that the world has created for us and unfortunately, we compare how we measure up to that, rather than what the Lord has said over us. We are often caught in the 'hamster wheel' of performance rather than being in the rest of relationship.

That is what happened in David's family when the prophet Samuel came to anoint the next king. Jessie, David's father, presented what looked good on the outside. As a father, he compared his children and judged them by his own ideas. He thought he knew what God wanted, by presenting what he was most proud of.

But the Lord said to Samuel, "Do not look at his appearance or at his physical stature, because I have refused him. For the Lord does not see as man sees; for man looks at the outward appearance, but the Lord looks at the heart."

1 Samuel 16:7

Zacchaeus up a tree (Luke 19) is another great example. The world's narration over his life wrote him off as a thief, a man unworthy of relationship and connection. Zacchaeus was betraying Jewish culture and life by being a corrupt tax collector. Jesus saw his heart and knew that he was only one encounter away from transformation.

When the Lord looks at us, what He speaks over us is so different from what we think and expect.

Reflection

- Take a moment to record the many ways the Lord speaks uniquely to you.

- Throughout the day, tune into an awareness of His presence, and recognise when He is trying to get your attention; either to show His love for you or someone else. Journal your experience.

- How is the Lord wanting to love you today?

Thy word is a lamp unto my feet, and a light unto my path

Day 01 / Growing.

When Gary & I met, Gary had a thick Welsh accent. I couldn't understand him on the phone and struggled when we were in person because I wasn't tuned to hearing his accent.

In the first few years of marriage, we faced some miscommunication. Phrases we used had different implications as a result of our different upbringings. Gary would say "I'll be there now." Unfortunately, it took me a long time to understand that "I'll be there now" didn't mean 'immediately'; it meant I'll be there somewhere between five minutes and two hours.

The only way we overcame this language barrier was to spend time together.

Developing skills in hearing God's voice takes time and practice. In the same way, building muscle requires lifting little weights first, rather than trying to go straight to lifting 20kg (44 pounds).

In Australia, we have an advert that says "from little things, big things grow."

This is true with hearing His voice and developing a prophetic lifestyle. We must start somewhere. Even if you feel super confident in hearing the Lord, growth requires consistent practice and engagement with Him.

My sheep hear my voice-And I know them. John 10:27

He wants to spend time with you so much more than you can comprehend. He calls you friend and desires to share what is on His heart.

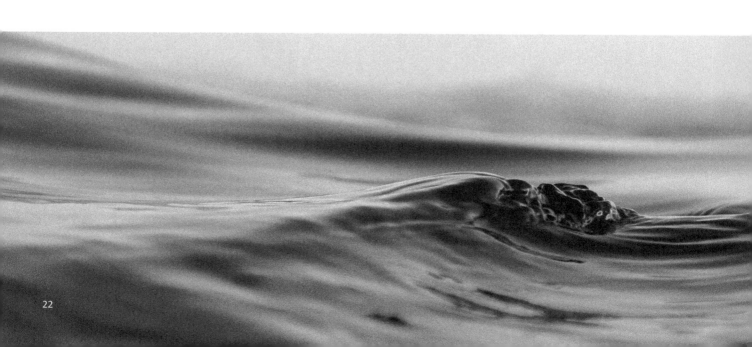

Blessed is the one who listens to me watching daily at my gates, waiting beside my doors.
Proverbs 8:34

We can get easily discouraged by comparing our walk with the Lord, to others. How we see, hear and communicate with Him isn't like the person next door!

In the same way, just like we have four seasons in a year; know you are walking in different places, called for different purposes; walking with different people groups, all to make the name of Jesus famous. Only you can express the heart of God as you do. Only you can walk your road with him.

If you have found yourself in a place of comparison, why not pray this prayer today.

Lord I give up the lie of comparison. Comparison you have no hold over me, no longer can you affect my relationship with the Lord. I receive Your grace and the ability to go on my journey and build my relationship with the Lord.

Reflection

- Start this time by being thankful for the ways the Lord speaks uniquely to you from Week 1, Day 3.

- In the context of your spiritual journey, write down 1 area you would like to see growth in.

- Ask the Lord to share what His heart is for your journey and relationship with Him through this next season.

"Confidence is walking into
a room and not comparing
myself to another."

Day 02 /
Journaling.

The four steps to Hearing God's Voice:
1. Quiet down
2. Fix your eyes on Jesus
3. Tune into spontaneous thoughts
4. Write it down

Growing in hearing God for yourself can be a big challenge. Self doubt and analytical thinking can get in the way. It aborts spontaneous flow and it causes us to doubt what the Lord says about us and to us.

However, one of the easiest ways around this is to journal. Journaling with the Lord is to follow step number four - Write it down.

Even though the first 3 steps still apply; making space to record your interactions and two-way conversation allows time and connection to happen, and also helps to disconnect our logical thoughts.

It enables us to hone our skills in hearing His voice and grow our ability to discern what is His voice and what is our own. Another great advantage of journaling is the ability to reflect on what we have 'heard' and hence written. This enables us to take the time to not only process but to weigh it. When we record God's voice through journaling, it removes the pressure to weigh the word in the moment so that we can revisit it without interrupting the spontaneous flow.

Journaling with the Lord; it is best used in the context of relationship rather than accessing revelation. Most of our journaling is for our personal edification, comfort and growth. God loves to spend time with you and to talk to you about deep things that are on His heart and yours. Just like a friend it becomes a recorded two way conversation that is penned for you to grow, trust and connect in.

———

I will write your words on the tablets of my heart. I will meditate on them day and night.

Psalm 119:1

Reflection

As you head into this wonderful journey of discovering God's heart for you, take time to ask him questions and then allow him to respond. Seek His heart and be in His presence. If it helps, put on some quiet worship music and you can begin with asking the Lord this question:

- What do you love most about your relationship with me? Write down His response.

Day 03 / Whose voice?

We are often taught to place a higher value on a word from someone else, unfortunately dismissing what or how He is speaking directly to us. We are so fearful of getting it wrong that we dismiss, downplay or doubt that we are hearing Him ourselves.

The big question often is, whose voice am I hearing? Is it me—Is it God—or is it the enemy?

The apostle Paul indicates that we have a responsibility to consider what we hear from the Lord carefully. We are to hold onto what is good and let go of what isn't.

1 Thessalonians 5:20-21 | "Do not despise prophecies. Test all things; hold fast what is good."

When we approach hearing His voice with the lens of learning, we will avoid the snare of having to be 100% correct. It is a joy to grow and learn, rather than being terrorised by the fear of missing it. It is unwise to think that we can hear 100% accurately 100% of the time. We must be aware that we only see in part.

The New Testament is crystal clear; it is imperative to weigh prophecy. It is our responsibility to weigh what we hear for ourselves and what we receive from others.

1 Corinthians 14:29 | "Let two or three prophets speak, and let the others, judge."

How do I grow in discerning God's voice?

Here are five keys

1. Scripture
We need to make sure we have a foundation in the word of God - the Bible. You can ask yourself this question: does it line up with the word of God? The written word is our first measurement in discerning His voice. It is likened to the fireplace and fire. Fire in a fireplace is safe, warm, inviting and creates an ability to feast. Fire without a fireplace is dangerous.

If you want to grow in the Rhema word (spoken word) dive into the Logos - the written word.

2. The nature of God

Exodus 34:6 | And the Lord passed before him and proclaimed, "The Lord, the Lord God, merciful and gracious, long-suffering, and abounding in goodness and truth."

When we search out scripture we see His character and nature. We discover that He is a loving Father full of mercy and grace. He is not angry and controlling but invites us to experience His ways and abundant life.

When you are testing what you hear, ask: Does it sound condemning, critical and shaming? Or does it sound like life? Is it peace? Is it supernatural wisdom?

3. The inner witness

Even if what you hear, seems to be from the Lord based on Points 1 & 2, you should also have an inner witness of agreement with what you are hearing.

1 John 2:27. "But the anointing which you have received from Him abides in you, and you do not need that anyone teach you; but as the same anointing teaches you concerning all things, and is true, and is not a lie, and just as it has taught you, you will abide in Him."

Remember, we need other people's input, as well as having our internal checks.

4. Good Fruit

When we have a word from the Lord, it will always produce fruit. Have you done a fruit inspection? What is the flavour that you are left with?

James 3:17 | "But the wisdom that is from above is first pure, then peaceable, gentle, willing to yield, full of mercy and good fruits, without partiality and without hypocrisy."

Does it reflect the fruit of the spirit?

Galatians 5:22 | "But the fruit of the Spirit is love, joy, peace, long-suffering, kindness, goodness, faithfulness"

What you hear from the Lord will always produce good fruit.

5. Community

Proverbs 27:17 | "As iron sharpens iron, so one person sharpens another."

There is victory in the council of many. Many does not mean everyone. Find people in your life that you respect and trust. Ask them to prayerfully consider the word. They will see something from a different perspective. It is so healthy to hear from people that love you and want the best from you, even if they don't always agree!

Feedback from others helps us grow. It can be vulnerable and scary, however it is worth the reward!

Reflection

- Tune into the Lord and ask one or all of the questions below. Journal your answers.

  - What are some of your favourite things about me?
  - What did you enjoy watching me do today/yesterday?
  - How would you like to encourage me today?
  - Is there a promise you want to remind me of?

- Using the 4 points above, weigh and process what you've written.

- Sit in His presence and allow Him to fill you with His love, strength, comfort, and peace.

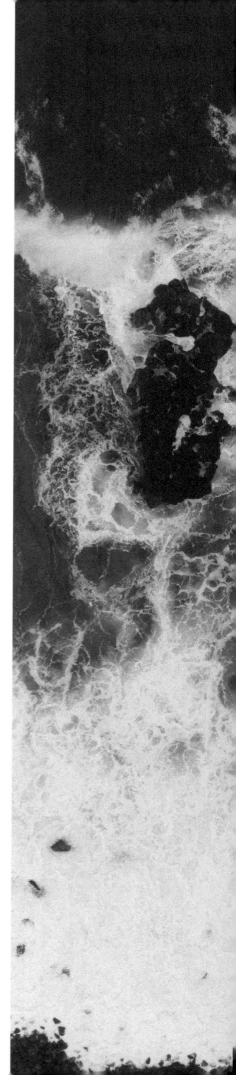

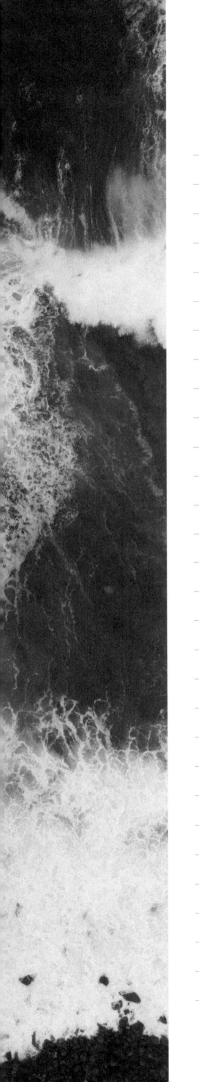

Day 04 /
Abiding in Him.

———

If you abide in Me, and My words abide in you, you will ask what you desire, and it shall be done for you. By this My Father is glorified, that you bear much fruit; so you will be My disciples. As the Father loved Me, I also have loved you; abide in My love. If you keep My commandments, you will abide in My love, just as I have kept My Father's commandments and abide in His love. These things I have spoken to you, that My joy may remain in you, and that your joy may be full. This is My commandment, that you love one another as I have loved you. Greater love has no one than this, than to lay down one's life for his friends. You are My friends if you do whatever I command you. No longer do I call you servants, for a servant does not know what his master is doing; but I have called you friends, for all things that I heard from My Father I have made known to you.

John 15:7-15

Friendship and relationship takes time and effort. No one can do it for you. What is abiding and how do I do it?

To abide means "to accept and/or act in accordance with." Simply put, abiding with Him, means:

- accepting all that He has given you
- accepting all that He says about you
- acting in accordance with His ways

Jesus gives a commandment to "love as I have loved you." (John 13:34) Most of us would quote this verse from the Old Testament where it says to love your neighbour as yourself. How many of us are good at loving ourselves? I want to propose that we are terrible at it. Here, Jesus is saying, "abide in me—receive and accept My love for you. It is only then that you are able to give it away." His love covers. His love is unconditional. His love is unrelenting. His love is full of grace and truth.

Reflection

Pray this prayer:

"Lord, thank You for all that You have given me. Help me today and each day forward, to know how to accept and receive Your unconditional and unrelenting love; that I may be able to learn to love like You love me."

Take some time to abide in Him and journal your thoughts. You may like to start by asking the Lord: In what ways have You shown me that You love me?

Day 05 /
Comfort.

_____

All praises belong to the God and Father of our Lord Jesus Christ. For he is the Father of tender mercy and the God of endless comfort. He always comes alongside us to comfort us in every suffering so that we can come alongside those who are in any painful trial. We can bring them this same comfort that God has poured out upon us.

2 Corinthians 1:3-4

Faith begins at the end of our ability and comfort zone. When the global crisis hit, it popped the false bubble that we are in control of our own lives. With everything suddenly changing, and the situation still ever-evolving, it requires us to live by faith and not by sight. It took me so many years to understand that faith isn't risk. It is simply trusting in a good, good Father.

Even when I don't like what's happening—when I'm left in a place of wondering, "why?", I know that He is good. I lean into who He is, reminding myself that I can trust Him to make everything work to my benefit. He is more than worthy to be trusted!

In all the places I experience suffering and pain, He is there with endless comfort. He will always be there to encourage, comfort and strengthen.

His promises are true; they are 'Yes and Amen!'

"Do you know Him as comforter?"

Reflection

As you spend time with the Lord:

- Write down three miracles that you need (one each of, emotional, physical and spiritual).
- Ask the Lord how you can be on the look out for His presence and how He is working in your life today.
- Ask the Lord for a picture that describes the way in which He brings comfort to you.

And those who know Your name will put their trust in You; For You, Lord, have not forsaken those who seek You.

Psalm 9:10

ABIDING

3

Day 01 /
Grace and Truth.

The grace of the Lord is typically expressed or defined as "unmerited favour, undeserved blessing." While that is true, it is only true in part. His grace is also a "supernatural influence upon a person's life." We see this time and time again through the lives of people: grace to be someone that they thought was impossible, grace to live a different way, grace to be apart of the family of God.

We love the letter of the law. We also love to hold others accountable to the "right and wrong" standards that only we have created. Even though it makes us feel better or more powerful, Jesus came with grace. His standards of truth remained the same, but He did it in the most contrasting way. It was contrary to the religious and cultural way.

The tool He used to reach hearts was always grace. He said to the woman who was caught in adultery, "go and sin no more"(John 8:11)." He didn't pretend her sin didn't exist, He covered it and gave her the grace to go a different way.

And of His fullness we have all received, and grace for grace. For the law was given through Moses, but grace and truth came through Jesus Christ.

John 1:16-17

Jesus came to earth and was definitely not what they were expecting and wanting. They wanted a saviour who was a warrior to defeat their enemy. During the time of Jesus, they were under the rule of the Roman empire. Although culture said to hate your enemy, Jesus said to love and serve your enemy.

God is not a God who sits on the throne absent from you. He is a Father who wants you to encounter the grace in which Jesus came with. It is a grace that surpasses your understanding or level of "deservedness." It is the grace to know that your past doesn't hold you prisoner nor does your present dictate your future.

He wants you to receive the truth that will set you free. It's not something that is shoved down your throat like the worst veggies you ate as a kid. His truth is always served on a platter of grace; for you to simply receive and be free.

Reflection

Put on some worship music and spend some time sitting with the Lord.

- Allow His grace to disrupt your thinking and your hiding places.
- Allow His grace to wash you with the truth of how He really thinks about you.
- Allow His grace to cover you.
- Allow His grace to adopt you into his family.
- Allow His grace to heal the parts of your heart that are broken.
- Allow His enabling grace to transform you.

Journal your experience.

Day 02 /
In tune.

No amount of gifting can take the place of Love. Jesus laid down His life in love. He asks us to do the same.

When we are learning and growing in the gifts, we need to be grounded in His love. You have heard us say, "you can't give what you don't have." We need to receive, not just convince ourselves mentally, that we are loved. We need to continually encounter His love for us so we can walk in it.

———

Though I speak with the tongues of men and of angels, but have not love, I have become a clanging symbol.

1 Corinthians 13:1

In 1 Corinthians 13, Paul starts speaking loudly about love. You will notice however, he talks about gifts in the previous chapter and he jumps right back into gifts after talking about love.

Why? It is a pattern in scripture.

Another place in scripture we see clanging symbols is in Exodus 28:33-34 "And beneath upon the hem of it and you shall make pomegranates of blue, and of purple, and of scarlet, round about the hem thereof; and bells of gold between them round about: A golden bell and a pomegranate, a golden bell and a pomegranate, upon the hem of the robe round about."

The golden bells and pomegranate speak of sweet sounds and fragrant fruit-the bells are heard and the pomegranate is to be tasted. We understand that the bells speak of the calling of the believer whilst the pomegranate speaks of the conduct of the believer, the fruit of their life.

Can you see the pattern?
1 Corinthians 12 - Gifts : Bell
1 Corinthians 13 - Love : Fruit
1 Corinthians 14 - Gifts : Bell

Now returning to 1 Corinthians, Paul expresses that if you have a room full of gifted people without love, it represents two bells clanging together. This produces competition, comparison, insecurity and the like. However, with the appropriate fruit of love in between, the bells make beautiful music.

He so beautifully wants to encourage us, to have love. As long as we have love in between, we can have the gifts working together to express the fragrance of Christ.

"He wants to encourage us, to have love."

Reflection

Take some time to still your thoughts, put on some worship music and rest in His presence. Ask for His tangible presence and love to fill you.

- Ask Him to share with you the extent of His love for you.
- Ask the Lord how you are called to show love in your community.
- Journal your experience and the expression of His heart towards you.

Day 03 /
A puzzle piece.

Have you ever done a massive puzzle? When you start, pieces are everywhere, with no obvious purpose or position. It's not until you sort things out, that you can start to gain perspective on how it all fits together.

The prophetic often reminds me of a puzzle. God has the big picture in His heart. He knows what He has to work with; He knows the story of our lives. He knows what he has called us to; He has gone before us!

Sometimes when we can't see where we are going or how situations will unfold, He reveals His heart through the prophetic, which adds colour and new dimensions to our perspective. He uses the prophetic to enable us to align with His perspective and develop part of the picture one piece at a time.

Trusting Him with the big picture can be easier said than done. Often we try to figure it all out. We try to fit our personal words together to see how they are going to connect. We can often get disappointed in our futile efforts and unmet expectations.

———

For we know in part and we prophesy in part. But when that which is perfect hascome, then that which is in part will be done away.

1 Corinthians 13:9

It is not our job to make sure everything fits together. We don't have to see it all, know the big picture, or have it all together. We simply see in part. It's God's job to know everything. He sees the beginning, the end, and all the in-betweens. He takes what we think is unclear or useless and he moulds it into a stunning whole.

God is our master painter and He is outworking His workmanship in your life.

We are all on a journey. We have the privilege of being encouraged and to encourage, to strengthen and to be strengthened, to comfort and to be comforted.

Each piece of your life and calling may not make sense right now, or you may not have a clue how God can take what you have to offer and make something beautiful.

Allow Him to speak into your heart today and know that He treasures the puzzle pieces of your life and that He is faithful to complete the good work He has started.

He is the master potter and you are the clay
Isaiah 64:8

Reflection

Spend some time with the Lord.

- What are some practical ways in which you can learn to trust Him with the big picture?

- Ask him to show you a picture of how He sees you, the significance you hold in His heart and in His kingdom family. Write or draw what He reveals to you.

- Ask Him to give you a promise that you can hold onto for this season.

"...God can take what you have to offer and make something beautiful."

Day 04 /
Community.

When we are growing in the prophetic it is imperative to understand that this gift in the new covenant is meant for community. It is to be weighed by others; for in the counsel of many, there is victory. As discussed yesterday, we all need each other. We all see in part and play a part.

Read Exodus 17:12-14.
We read that as Moses lifted his hands, he would be winning the battle. So when he got tired Aaron and Hur helped hold his hands.

We need others to believe the very things that God has for us when we don't have the faith. We need Aarons and Hurs in our lives to call the gold out of us-to remind us of who we are in Christ.

Brené Brown puts our need for community in such a beautiful way.

> "A deep sense of love and belonging is an irreducible need of all people. We are biologically, cognitively, physically, and spiritually wired to love, to be loved, and to belong. When those needs are not met, we don't function as we were meant to. We break. We fall apart. We numb. We ache. We hurt others. We get sick."

"Carry each others burdens and in this way you will fulfil the law of Christ." | Galatians 6:2

If one part suffers, every part suffers with it; if one part is honoured every part rejoices with it.

1 Corinthians 12:26

There is so much power in carrying each others' burdens. Equally, there is so much power in celebrating each others' over-comings, promotions and victories.

"As iron sharpens iron, so one person sharpens another." | Proverbs 27:17

Power in community is displayed when we realise that we each have great strengths to support one another; where one is weak, the others have the strength to equip and support.

"We need others to believe... To call out the gold..."

Reflection

- Do you have a community around you? If not, ask the Lord to highlight a group of people that you can begin to grow and develop trust with. A place where you are equally challenged and encouraged, eg. a church community or a friendship group.

- Ask the Lord to highlight one person in your community. Speak to Him about one way you can encourage, comfort and strengthen them this week and then activate it.

- Reflect on your experience.

Day 05 /
Out doing one another.

Accountability is a lifeline that we miss in fear of being shamed, judged and rejected. We are often taught that it is our sin, mistakes and struggles that we need to be accountable for. We forget that it is also about being accountable for the greatness that is inside of us. We need to be accountable for the "awesome" moments when we didn't "stuff it up" and the grace of God was flowing.

———

And let us consider how we may spur one another on toward love and good deeds, not giving up meeting together, as some are in the habit of doing, but encouraging

Hebrews 10:24-25

Our ultimate goal of accountability is to love well and do the good deeds that Jesus designed us for. It feels like this scripture is almost saying, "Hey! If you want to compete at anything, compete in this..."

Let's face it, we all go through "seasons of stupidity." Being reminded of the fact that there is life beyond it—it is just a season, and not who we are—is so powerful. This is healing, this is redeeming, this is hope—this is community. To be spurred on towards love and good deeds makes you want to do them more. To be seen, valued, and encouraged makes all the difference.

When you have had the opportunity to be on the receiving end of such community encouragement, there is only a greater appreciation and value for what it means to be the one to encourage. When you get to spur on and encourage someone towards all that God's called them to be, you may just have the key that unlocks their heart. It can shift their heart and mind towards that which the Lord says and thinks about them.

Accountability is a necessity to grow in maturity and to be transformed into the likeness of Christ.

Reflection

- What do you feel the Lord is speaking to you personally in regard to accountability?

- Who are the people in your community that the Lord is highlighting for you to spur on and encourage? What are some of the practical ways that you can apply this?

- Are there specific people in your community with whom you can be accountable with? If not, ask the Lord to show you who could help you grow in your journey.

When You said, "Seek My face," My heart said to You, "Your face, Lord, I will seek."

Psalm 27:8

HEART

4

Day 01 /
Faithfulness.

The Father's perspective is different to ours. We, like so many in the bible, can make excuses to the Lord. We tend to focus on our limitations rather than the possibilities that the Lord has for us. When we set our eyes on our limitations, we also limit what God can do in and through us. We manage our life by avoiding areas where we are afraid to trust Him.

It's amazing what fear does to us. It can literally cripple us. Imagine a man or woman in their early 60's- fit and vibrant, not old in any way. One day they have a bad fall. Though they fully recover, the fear of falling again has now gripped their heart. They no longer walk vibrantly; instead, they shuffle around like a very old person. This is irrespective to their ability to actually walk and go back to a "normal" life.

In the same way, fear and excuses cripple us. We walk around like a crippled person because we are fearful of our limitations. We are afraid of missing it or getting it wrong. When this happens, we miss the limitlessness of God.

———

Then the word of the Lord came to me, saying: Before I formed you in the womb I knew you; Before you were born I sanctified you; I ordained you a prophetto the nations. Then said I: Ah, Lord God! Behold, I cannot speak, for I am a youth.

Jeremiah 1:4-6

Jeremiah gave the excuse that he was too young. Moses gave the excuse for his inability to speak. I am surprised he didn't just say "Look, I murdered someone. You can't use me!" Gideon gave the excuse that he was the least of his clan. The list of people who had valid reasons or limitations continues, but they then chose to believe God and what He had to say.

———

Moreover the word of the Lord came to me, saying, Jeremiah, what do you see? And I said, I see a branch of an almond tree. Then the Lord said to me, You have seen well, for I am ready to perform My word.

Jeremiah 1:11-12

Here we see the Lord teaching Jeremiah a simple lesson—being faithful with what he saw. If Jeremiah simply looked at what God was showing him, his excuse would melt away.

It is a valuable lesson for us-just agree and be faithful with what He says about you and with what He shows you. He has the big picture in His heart!

As we grow in the prophetic, there are times we can feel silly. Perhaps because we see differently or because we perceive that what we have received is generic or too simple. Whatever you qualify as your limitations; know that the Lord just wants you to be faithful with what He has for you.

Reflection

- Have you given God excuses as to why you can't or won't agree with what He says about you?

- What are some of the excuses that you have given God?

- Ask the Lord about them and how He wants to reset your mindset regarding these excuses.

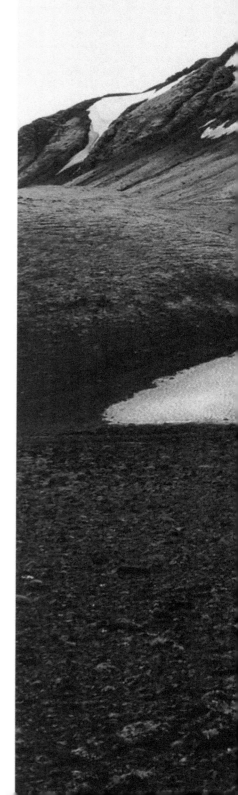

Day 02 /
Can it live?

The prophetic is the only gift that has an immediate effect upon a person's heart and atmosphere. A word from the Father changes everything.

The most beautiful thing about the prophetic is that it speaks life. Positive prophetic affirmation causes destiny activation. We are in such need of comfort, encouragement and strength as we face each day in this rapidly changing world.

We can view things with our natural understanding and speak what is "positive," but when the words of the Lord are heard, it carries creative tangible life with it.

_____

And He said to me, Son of man, can these bones live?

So I answered, O Lord God, You know. Again He said to me, Prophesy to these bones, and say to them, O dry bones, hear the word of the Lord! Thus says the Lord God to these bones: Surely I will cause breath to enter into you, and you shall live. I will put sinews on you and bring flesh upon you, cover you with skin and put breath in you; and you shall live. Then you shall know that I am the Lord

Ezekiel 37:3-5

When He speaks into our hearts, He brings life to the things that we think are dead by breathing His life back into them.

Sometimes we go through circumstances and situations where we feel like what was in our hearts has died. The hope we had is now gone. We are afraid to believe that He can still do what He has promised, especially when it isn't looking how we expected. In these moments, people may even voice their opinions and agree with what seems dead, while Jesus is actually in the midst of speaking life into our hearts and lives.

Following Jesus isn't as simple as a path that takes us from A-Z. Trusting him can feel like we are on the wildest roller coaster! Often our journey starts at A then takes us to D-G-B. It is completely illogical. However, He makes everything beautiful in its time.

_____

And we know that all things work together for good to those who love God, to those who are the called according to His purpose.

Romans 8:28

Reflection

- Ask the Lord to show you areas that He would like to bring alive in your heart once again.

- What are the words of life that the Lord wants to speak to you today?

- Spend some time in His presence, allowing His words to refresh you and breathe life into your heart.

Day 03 /
Servanthood.

Jesus came to serve us and show us a better way-a way to live according to His kingdom. It is better than anything we can conjure up or create for ourselves. His intention from the beginning has always been to have us live in communion with Him-this is made possible through our adoption as sons and daughters.

———

But as many as received Him, to them He gave the right to become children of God, to those who believe in His name.
John 1:12

Jesus was made manifest to destroy the works of the enemy (1 John 3:8). He did this through the vehicle of servanthood. He demonstrated the authority of the kingdom by serving mankind. He laid down his life to pay the price of redemption. He has given us the authority of the kingdom, to do the same. He has given us His grace to love and serve our world.

The way Jesus displayed leadership was opposite to what we expect of leaders today. So many people missed the fact that he was messiah and king because they were looking through the lens the world had provided.

Jesus said, "I am the way, the truth, and the life. No one comes to the Father except through me." John 14:6

He demonstrated what we are to follow.

———

But Jesus called them to Himself and said, "You know that the rulers of the Gentiles lord it over them, and those who are great exercise authority over them. Yet it shall not be so among you; but whoever desires to become great among you, let him be your servant. And whoever desires to be first among you, let him be your slave-just as the Son of Man did not come to be served, but to serve, and to give His life a ransom for many.

Matthew 20:25-28

———

Jesus, knowing that the Father had given all things into His hands, and that He hadcome from God and was going to God, rose from supper and laid aside His garments, took a towel and girded Himself. After that, He poured water into a basin and began to wash the disciples' feet, and to wipe them with the towel with which He was girded.

John 13:3-5

Jesus said that if you want to be the greatest—you must be the servant of all.

Through the prophetic, we get to serve those around us with solutions that wouldn't be possible otherwise. We get to have access to the "God option" in any given circumstance. It is such an honour to be able to express the heart of God to someone and watch how it impacts their hearts. We know that God goes to great lengths to express His love—He finds us!

———

Whoever says he abides in him ought to walk in the same way in which he walked.

1 John 2:6

Reflection

Often we pursue recognition of our greatness to affirm our identity. However, Jesus says that we will be great by laying this down and serving others, because the identity of the kingdom is servanthood. While the desire for greatness can be pure, any pursuit of greatness that denies servanthood is what we want to guard our hearts from. Let's ask God to "search our hearts" today.

- Ask the Holy Spirit to speak to you about how He has designed your prophetic gift to serve the body.

- Once you have done this, ask the Holy Spirit to reveal to you any places that your desire for greatness may be greater than your willingness to serve. Ask Him to speak to you about these areas.

- Spend some time with the Lord and ask Him to help you align yourself with the servanthood of Jesus.

Day 04 /
Awakening.

"Lazarus, Come Out."

These few words were said by Jesus in John 11:43 as He stood in front of an open tomb, surrounded by a crowd of people and the smell of a four-day-old decomposing body filling the air.

Jesus approached the tomb of His dear friend Lazarus with the full assurance that the Father was with Him. He purposely made mention of His Father's presence by giving thanks, wilfully making the statement that the dead man lying in the tomb in front of Him was going to come alive again because He (Jesus) was truly the sent Son of God. Jesus' intention that day was not only to awaken Lazarus, but also the crowd of spectators. He was going to shatter their unbelief and gift them the opportunity to believe in Him, just as Martha, Mary, and Lazarus did, by demonstrating His authority over death itself.

We are much like the characters of this story-we need an awakening. Perhaps it is an initial awakening of our hearts coming alive to the realisation that Jesus Christ is our saviour, healer and deliverer. Perhaps it's

to awaken us to an awareness of all that He is, and is capable of. Whichever it is, we are all invited into a place of ongoing awakening.

Awakening is "an act or moment of suddenly becoming aware of something" or "an act of waking from sleep." The characters surrounding Jesus all experienced this, some for the first time and others repeatedly.

Jesus extends an invitation for not only Lazarus' heart to be made physically alive, but for others who witnessed the resurrection to experience their own "resurrection of heart and spirit." Hope walked amongst the people through Jesus. He was showing Himself as the answer to their complete awakening.

After Jesus called Lazarus, the once dead man walked out, still wrapped in His grave clothes. At the instruction of Jesus, the grave clothes were taken off. It is imperative that when we wake up to a new reality in Jesus, we leave the past in the past. God wants to resurrect your heart and clothe you with righteousness (Isaiah 61:10).

Reflection

- Put yourself in the narrative of the story. Who do you best relate to and why?

- What areas of your life do you feel need to be awakened or re-awakened? Spend some time with Jesus to find out what they are. Through your process of discovery, identify the areas of the past that are ready to be left in the past.

- How do you feel Jesus wants to awaken others through your relationship with Him?

Awakens us to awareness of all that He is.

Day 05 / Burning.

Spending time in the Word of God can seem dry at times even though we know that it is good for us. However, when we do spend time reading the Word, we are opened to the revelation of who Christ is and the Word becomes alive.

That He might sanctify and cleanse her with the washing of water by the word.

Ephesians 5:26

Read Luke 23:13-35
The 'Road to Emmaus' Bible story: two men are travelling to Emmaus just days after the crucifixion of Jesus when a third man "drew near to them." They walked and discussed the life of Jesus of Nazareth and considered, He may still be alive after His tomb was found empty. When the men get to Emmaus and join in supper they recognised Jesus as He broke and blessed the bread. Jesus then disappeared, and the two men returned to Jerusalem where they proclaim to the "Eleven" that the Lord has risen!

They reflected upon their time with Jesus after He disappeared and said to each other "Were not our hearts burning within us while he talked with us on the road and opened the Scriptures to us? (Luke 24:32)

Revelation of Jesus causes our hearts to burn.

Jesus is the Word! "The Word became flesh and dwelt among us." | John 1:14a

The revelation of Jesus causes our hearts to burn. Jesus himself took them through Scripture. We couldn't ask for a better teacher than the Word himself.

Interestingly, it was as they were having fellowship that Jesus chose to disclose Himself to them. It is significant that it is around the supper table that the disciples' eyes are opened and they see Jesus for who He really is. After the resurrection, many of the appearances of Jesus are associated with table fellowship. This is true in Luke 24:41-43, Acts 1:4, and in John 21:9-15. In the intimacy of fellowship, Jesus reveals Himself to us. His working in our lives becomes clearer; His provision and protection comes into focus.

It is also important to note, that when the disciples recognised Jesus, He disappeared. Fellowship with Him was not going to depend on their ability to see Him, but rather upon their ability to take Him at His word.

Reflection

Building rhythms into your daily life can help to provide opportunities for you to bring focus, to connect and to commune with the Father.

- What is a practical time that you can set aside to read the Word and journal?

- Is there a special place that helps you to connect with Him? If no, why not create a space? ie. a favourite chair or corner, a place with a window for you to look out at nature.

- If you have been feeling dry, take this time to sit in His presence and ask the Lord to refresh and renew your heart today.

- Set aside some time this week to take communion together with friends or family members.

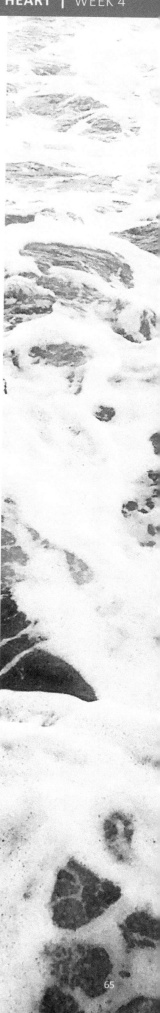

Ask, and it will be given to you;
seek, and you will find; knock,
and it will be opened to you.

Matthew 7:7

5

Day 01 /
Father's Heart.

One of the greatest parables to describe the heart of God our Father, is seen in Luke 15:11-32. It is titled in most bibles, "The Prodigal Son," persuading us to look at the narrative through the experience of the younger son, who rebelled against his dad and left home to squander his inheritance. However, what does it look like from the perspective of the Father?

I believe his heart yearned for his son to be present in his home, a place of safety and provision. He didn't want him to live carelessly, giving in to his own unhealthy desires, but instead wanted him to thrive in the best place he had built for him.

The father's house was not just a place of provision and protection (vs.14,17). It was also a place of output and labour (vs.17, 25, 29). What would be built under the father's care and oversight was going to benefit his sons for far longer than their own lifetime (v.31). Perhaps the younger son wanted to do things his own way and grew weary of the restraints and toil. He asked for his share of the inheritance, but didn't have the maturity to manage it (v.13).

Perhaps the father knew that this was a disaster in the making and after he left, maybe even waited for him every day with the longing that he would return (v.19). The story tells us how the father spotted the son coming back "from a great way off" his son, however, was returning hungry, dirty, and barefoot (v.22). The love of the father so outweighed the ignorance and the rebellion of the son that his compassionate nature was ignited upon the very glimpse of Him; he "ran and fell on his neck and kissed Him (v.20)."

He looked beyond his rebellion and wasn't offended by his stench. He didn't focus on the loss of money and property and he wasn't worried about his own pristine robes being stained by the mud and dust the prodigal brought with him. His son was home. His most precious asset came back with the recognition that to be with his dad and in his care is incomparable to any other place.

This dad is a representation of our Heavenly Father and His heart towards us, His children.

...the kindness of His heart cannot be fully fathomed.

Maybe we can recognise ourselves as the prodigal in some ways. When we stray and find our way back to God, it would be enough for Him to only say, "welcome home" but the love of the Father and the kindness of His heart cannot be fully fathomed. "The LORD is compassionate and gracious, slow to anger, abounding in love (Psalm 103:8)."

He would do to us as the father in the parable did for his son. What a beautiful picture of immediate promotion upon repentance of his boy. The father made his servants dress the once wavered boy and he gave him a ring that entitled him to the provisions and benefits of the house once again. Like the son, we are celebrated for our return to the Father's heartland; for it is where He is that we find life (v.24).

Reflection

- In what ways can you relate to the prodigal son in this story?
- What ungodly beliefs hinder you from knowing His heart?
- What has God revealed to you about His heart for you through this parable?

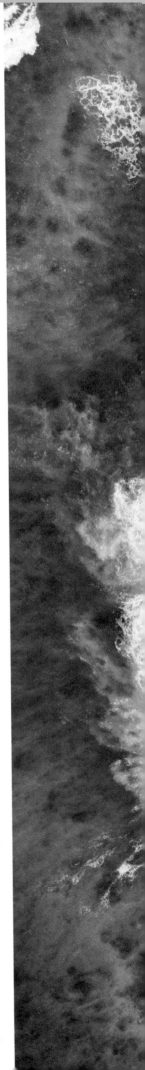

Day 02 /
Disappointment.

King David knew what is was to feel as though He had disappointed God and to feel like God had disappointed Him.

David was found and summoned by the Prophet Samuel from the middle of a field, while he was alone and unseen by others. He was anointed and then eventually appointed King over the very land where he used to shepherd. David was chosen by God. He was picked and appointed because God knew his potential, created him for a divine purpose, and knew that he would be an individual who trusted his creator.

King David was also familiar with failure. He betrayed his close friend and his defender Uriah by sleeping with his wife and then had him killed to cover up the shame of impregnating her.

Like David, we are not picked and appointed by God because of our perfection. Instead, God looks for what He saw in the king he appointed; that is, a repentant and dependant heart (2 Samuel 12:13).

We do not need to allow the shame of our wrongdoings to demote the Father's position in our lives. Our disappointment does not un-appoint Jesus as the King of our heart; He is not that easily demoted. However, we do have a choice whether or not we allow ourselves to withdraw from Him. Just remember-God willingly invites us to draw close in these times, despite our greatest weaknesses, and even if we feel clothed in our ugliest forms of shame.

David also felt let down, forgotten, and disappointed by God at times (Psalm13:1-4). The enemy would love for us to think that God has wronged us and has intentionally disappointed us, leaving us alone to defend ourselves. If he can have us believe that this is true, we may lose trust in God, in the belief that God is truly good, and that He is working on behalf of us. It is in these times that we often lose hope. Sadly, some have bowed out of the race because they didn't comprehend the magnitude of just how much God is working all things out for our good (Romans 8:28).

If we give it enough time and submit to the process of being in relationship with Christ, we will get to see the things He has been working out behind the scenes come into the foreground. His goodness can't help but be seen in our lives. It will take a person willing to endure to see that He is a God that doesn't disappoint His children. We are invited to do what David did to position himself to witness just that—"my heart rejoices in your salvation. I will sing the Lord's praise, for he has been good to me." Psalm 13:4-5

I will lift up my eyes to the hills–From whence comes my help? My help comes from the Lord, Who made heaven and earth.

Psalm 121:1-2

Reflection

- Have you ever felt like you have disappointed God? If yes, in what ways?

- Have you ever felt like you were disappointed by God? If yes, in what ways?

- Spend some time hearing the redemptive thoughts of God towards you and His restorative thoughts about your relationship with Him.

Day 03 /
Forgiveness.

Our ultimate role model of how to live a life of forgiveness is Jesus Himself. The irony is, that He powerfully displayed it on His dying bed.

In Luke 23:34, we hear Him speak what we now recognise as some of the most famous words in Christendom. It was said during His crucifixion, while He was being pinned to a cross, scoffed at, and mocked while soldiers sat near His cross betting on His blood-stained garments. He prayed to the Father and asked what most of us would find hard to word in our best of times. He said, "Father, forgive them, for they know not what they do."

The word forgive in Luke (aphíēmi) means, "to let go, keep no longer, give up a debt, to depart from." He was asking the Father not to hold what they were doing against them, but instead to look away because He (Jesus) was the complete sacrifice for the mistakes they were making at that moment.

This is an ongoing challenge and example for us as children of God. Jesus modelled forgiveness and paid the price for forgiveness all at the same time. When we read over what He had to endure, it leaves us with little excuse not to forgive (to let go, to turn away). If God the Father can do it at the request of Jesus, so can we.

So the question remains-who is worthy of our forgiveness and who are we called to forgive?

The answer to this is once again found at the cross. Jesus did not discriminate who He died for (1 John 2:2), and He drew no boundary on the extent of that forgiveness (Matt 18:21-22). We, therefore, are compelled to follow the ultimate example of our role model.

Reflection

- Do you find it easy or difficult to forgive? Why do you think that is?

- Ask the Lord to show you if you are holding onto any unforgiveness towards a person. Take some time to process that with the Father. Allow Him to heal your heart as you forgive.

- A special part of the call to forgive is the need to forgive ourselves. Is there anything you need to forgive yourself for? Take some time with Jesus and allow Him to minister into these situations.

Day 04 / Shame.

"If you put shame in a Petri dish, it needs three things to grow exponentially: secrecy, silence and judgment. If you put the same amount of shame in a Petri dish and douse it with empathy, it can't survive," says Dr. Brené Brown in a follow up to her Ted talk on vulnerability.

Shame draws us away from connection. It is a powerful emotion that causes us to retreat into hiddenness. That drawing away causes us to live contrary to the way we have been created. Vulnerability is our path out of shame. However, that is a terrifying path most of the time.

Brené Brown defines vulnerability as "uncertainty, risk, and emotional exposure. But vulnerability is not weakness; it's our most accurate measure of courage."

As we discovered, Adam and Eve were the first to hide from God due to shame.

They encountered their nakedness and hid. We often do the same in our relationship with God. We hide areas of our hearts away from the light of His love.

For we do not have a High Priest who cannot sympathise with our weaknesses, but was in all points tempted as we are, yet without sin. Let us therefore come boldly to the throne of grace, that we may obtain mercy and find grace to help in time of need.

Hebrews 4:15-16

Jesus understands all that we go through. He is the best one to drown our shame with His empathy. He paid a high price for your shame-He took it; He bought it.

It doesn't matter what kind of shame it is. Whether it is your need for perfection or being stuck in receiving forgiveness for your past, He wants to hold your hand and lead your heart out of the prison of shame. His desire for you is freedom!

Reflection

- "Vulnerability is our path out of shame." What does this statement mean for you personally?

- Ask the Lord to reveal to you if there is an area of your life where you are currently in a 'prison' of shame?

- Invite the Lord into those areas of your life, allowing Him to speak love, truth, and wisdom. Process and discover with Him your journey towards freedom.

Day 05 /
Honesty & Trust.

Nelson Mandela, the great South African anti-apartheid revolutionary leader, stressed the importance of being "honest with ourselves" by acknowledging and taking into account our weaknesses and strengths. He suggests that it is from this place that "impact" is made. The Apostle Paul, another great leader, modelled this concept well; history tells us the mark he made through his life and writings.

We see this in 2 Corinthians 12:7-11 where Paul talks about the "thorn in his flesh." He recognises his own weakness and displays his vulnerable side by writing openly and honestly to the members of the Corinthian church, stating his struggle and need for relief. However, the passage also makes something else very evident-that Paul was honest with God. "Three times I pleaded with the Lord to take it away from me," he says. The word "pleaded" here, means, "I begged, I urged, I beseeched him." This emphasises his desperation and the strain this "thorn" was causing Paul's life and ministry. The Lord's reply was unique, however. He says, "

My grace is sufficient for you, for my power is made perfect in weakness." When Paul came before the Lord with such honesty, God, in return, gifted him with the promise of empowerment that was necessary for the impact of the gospel through his life and the security of his identity.

Paul wasn't dismissed by God because of his struggle. We, therefore, cannot be shy about what we are feeling or wrestling with, especially in front of God. We invite Him to journey with us and have Him view us in the most difficult of times. We see Jesus doing this when He prayed to the Father in Gethsemane right before He was crucified (Matthew 26:42). He said, "O my Father, if this cup may not pass away from me, except I drink it, your will be done." Jesus was in a state of anguish (Luke 22:44) over what He was about to have to endure, but He was laying His heart bare in front of His dad and he wasn't afraid to do so. Jesus modelled vulnerability, then went on to win our victory-what an amazing Saviour and example for our life! The Father wasn't about to demote Jesus or Paul (for that matter) and strip them of their mandate because they had some weak moments. In fact, this kind of honesty is exactly what God looks for to be in close relationship. The danger zone is when we think we can hide it from God.

...the importance of being honest with ourselves by acknowledging and taking into account our weaknesses and strengths.

Therefore, acknowledging weakness is necessary for our Christian growth and is an attribute of those who are pursuing integrity. The product of their pursuit is trustworthiness in relationships and partnerships. God is looking for us to be those people and He wants to provide those people for us. We all need people in our lives who are not afraid to be honest with themselves, about themselves, and honest with us about us. This kind of openness produces trust and strengthens relationship leading to an even greater impact for the Kingdom together, rather than independently (Deut 32:30).

Reflection

- Why do you think that honesty is necessary?

- Are there any areas of your life that you feel you need to be honest about with the Lord?
  - If yes, journal your thoughts with the Lord.
  - If you can't identify any, ask the Lord to show you anything that has gone unnoticed and process your thoughts with Him.

- Ask the Lord what His thoughts are towards you.

ENCOUNTERING

6

Day 01 /
He's a God of covenant.

Genesis 3:8 exhibits a stunning picture of the creator of the seas and stars who takes the time in the "cool of the day" to stroll through the picturesque landscape of Eden (Genesis 2). I don't believe it was uncommon for God to have had conversations with the other two beings He made, Man and Woman.

From the beginning, God intended deep connection with His unique creation and He cultivated it. It is evident here that Adam and Eve weren't just familiar with God's voice, but even the sound of His very footsteps; it implies that they knew their creator and their creator knew them.

Then came that very day-where they hid from God out of the shame and disobedience. Since then, humanity has ventured further and further away from that closeness that was once experienced with their Father.

The desire and nature of God has not altered, however, He is continuously drawing His creation back into a deep bond; He is giving opportunity for this connection by creating covenants.

When you sign up for a new car, you really don't need to get to know the salesman. All you want is the keys to your shiny new set of wheels and all he wants is the assurance that you can pay for it. Your credit history checks out, you sign on the dotted line, and you walk away. You may never know whether the salesman is married or what his hobbies are and he may never know that information about you. It's just a contract.

However, there is a vast difference between a contract and a covenant. In covenant, God gets to be Father, friend and everything else that He is. It is personal, intimate and interdependent. There is a mutual exchange of knowing and being known. We see this relationship throughout the Bible displayed through the 'heroes' of our faith. God chose them-He made a way for connection and expected a heart response. The beauty of the Gospel is that God made the way and gives us the free choice to reciprocate it or not. He made the covenant before we committed.

But God demonstrates His own love toward us, in that while we were still sinners, Christ died for us.

Romans 5:8

God wants to walk closely with you as He did with Adam in the garden. Your life may not look like an "Eden," but God is more than willing to journey with you through the mess and misery and bring about your victory. He paid for it-so why not walk in it?

The desire and nature of God has not altered...

Reflection

- Do you approach your relationship with God more like a contract or a covenant? In what ways?

- Ask God what the benefits of the New Covenant are for you, ie. emotionally, spiritually, physically and materially. Also ask Him to bring to memory any Scriptures that highlight this.

- Reflect on your own personal journey. Ask the Lord to show you and reveal to you His heart for you from the beginning up until the present and beyond. You may like to make it an extra special time with the Father and take communion in response.

Day 02 / Provider.

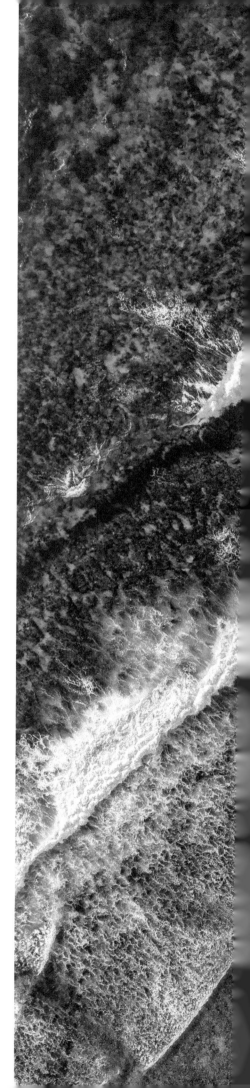

Whether you have had the privilege of giving birth to a child, being present at delivery or have just heard stories of deliveries; you would be aware that labour is not like a casual walk in a park. It's exhausting! Those first few moments seeing your child can be pure elation mixed with a deep desire for rest. For a mother, hearing the words "don't worry, it's my turn, now sleep", from a trusted individual, is just the invitation needed for her to instantly yield to the rest her body has been waiting for.

I propose that the Father is like these trusted individuals. Perhaps you have laboured and you feel exhausted by what you are facing and lack the strength to move further. God is calling you into a place of yielding to His provision and for you to allow Him to step in and relieve you of the pressure of doing it on your own.

You are invited into partnership with God (1 Cor 3:9) who provides in unique ways, but you aren't asked to completely abdicate your responsibility of what you are called to do. In the same way that a child is still a mother's responsibility, with the example above, a mother is simply yielding to what is better for both her and her child in that moment. We get to see the extent and magnitude of God's provision and intricate work in our lives when we trust what He says for us to do and then trust Him to do it (Mark 4:27-29).

God is calling you into a place of yeilding to His provision.

So how does God the provider partner with His people?

For some His provision may look like the widow who received the multiplication of her oil (2 Kings 4); her role was to try but trust. She had to action something by asking her neighbours for empty jars, she then poured the remaining oil into the provided jars and watched it multiply.

For others, it may look like a major stepping back from your duties and trusting that Jesus is doing the heavy lifting on your behalf. We see this in the story of Mary, Martha and their dead brother Lazarus (John 11).

Needless to say, what that situation needed was for Jesus to turn up. The two sisters may have assisted their brother when He was alive, but there was little they could do for him now. Their main part here was trust; much like the ravens mentioned in Luke 12:24, or like a new mother when she needs rest.

Your God is famously known as Jehovah Jireh. You can put your confidence in Him, believing that He will provide for your situation because He sees your need (Genesis 22).

Reflection

- Phil 4:19 says "And my God will supply every need of yours according to his riches in glory in Christ Jesus." What are you believing God for?

- Can you recall any stories where God has provided for you or others? Remind yourself and allow it to be a catalyst of faith in your heart.

- Think of a situation that you need to trust God for. Ask Him if there is any area that you are neglecting to partner with him in. How can you allow Him to partner with you through this?

Day 03 /
God of Peace.

There's a story of a couple who would jokingly chuckle and dance to an old song; the lyrics were, "I beg your pardon, I never promised you a rose garden." The wife looks at her husband with a confirming stare, saying, "That's right, it's been no walk in the park!" Her husband glances back replying, "I never told you it would be."

There is significance in the words of the husband above when you realise that these words had similarly been stated by Jesus when He called us to walk out our faith journey with Him. He said in John 16:33, "I have told you all this so that you may have peace in me. Here on earth you will have many trials and sorrows. But take heart, because I have overcome the world." Jesus didn't give us a false expectation that said, "Come to me and all your troubles will be over." He preempted the painful situations we would face with a promise that it would be accompanied by His presence.

Therefore, whatever comes against us can be overcome because He took the onslaught of our pain and turmoil on the cross and was victorious over it. The chastisement he faced "brought us peace" (Isaiah 53:5).

One of the most significant gifts of our salvation is peace. Jesus said, "I am leaving you with a gift-peace of mind and heart. And the peace I give is a gift the world cannot give. So don't be troubled or afraid." (John 14:27).

This word, "peace," used in both passages of John is translated in Greek as seirēnē. It is an action word that extends a call 'to join.' There is an invitation for us to come into union with the Prince of Peace himself, Jesus. He is the ultimate gift of peace to humanity (Luke 2:14) and the fullness of its expression is found, in Him (John 16:33). The peace that He personifies and the gift He extends is emphasised in Isaiah 53:5 with the Hebrew word šālôm; this means completeness, fulfilment, wholeness, healing, harmony, security, success, and prosperity. Peace, therefore, produces possibilities where there previously seemed to be none.

You may find yourself in the midst of calamity and your situation may be confusing. It is here that Jesus is opening His arms wide to you and His eyes beam with compassion, compelling you to walk and talk with Him. When you do so, you reside in peace; your heart and mind are filled with it; the atmosphere in and around you shifts. Why? because the Prince of Peace takes His throne in you and can't help but to stay close by you. Where He is, shalom reigns; it is a "realm where chaos is not allowed to enter" (P. D Hanson). Chaos is anything in your life that aims to violate or come against the nature, plan and purpose of a good God towards you.

He has called us to walk out our faith with Him...

Reflection

- What was your previous understanding of peace?

- What situations in your life require the Prince of Peace to step in?
  Take a moment to invite Him in.

- What was your experience with Jesus and what possibilities do you see in God now?

Day 04 /
God is our Shepherd.

Have you ever explored the profession of sheep rearing? The bible makes several references to Jesus as our Shepherd as we are His sheep. Perhaps it may be useful to understand what it is like so we can capture a little of what God is saying through the analogy.

To give you an idea:

- The days are long and the nights are short.
- You would be covered in dust most of the time.
- The weather would leave no compassion and would not be interested in negotiations.
- Sheep bite-a lot.
- Sheep make an annoying bleating sound and are prone to confusion.
- Sheep are usually the preferred meal for predators such as foxes, eagles, lions and bears.
- Sheep tend to wander off... often!

Reading through that list and realising that we are all still one of these sheep brings revelation of the need to know Jesus as our Good Shepherd.

If we didn't have a watchful and loving shepherd to look out for us, we would feel helpless. There will be times in life that we are confronted by our own humanity and how much we require someone bigger than ourselves to lead, guide, defend, and nurture us.

There are times we wander off course; it is then that we get to see the extravagant and kind heart of our shepherd, as he seeks to find us and carry us home. There is no shame in this, we aren't the first to wander off. Isaiah 53:6 describes the nation of Israel to be like sheep that have strayed away and left God's paths to follow their own. They desperately needed a shepherd; one who would rescue and save them, one who would help them find home and family again.

Jesus became this good shepherd (John 10:11) and modelled the compassionate and rescuing heart of His father so well. We see him sit amongst the despised of Jewish society in Luke 15:1-7. He sat willingly amongst "the tax collectors and sinners" and He spoke about a good shepherd who would not want one of His sheep to wander off and get lost. The heart He had for them is the same heart He has for you.

He is our Good Shepherd.

The revelation that He is a good and caring shepherd is necessary to hear His voice; for if we believe He is good, we will trust Him. When we allow ourselves to be so closely cared for by Him, we get to know the way He speaks. By doing so, we are not easily led astray by any other distraction or discouragement that comes along (John 10:4-5). Therefore, may you be encouraged to choose to position yourself in His presence, incline your ear to hear His heart often, and grow more confident in hearing His voice every day.

Reflection

- Has there been a time in your life that you have felt lost or have wandered away? How did Jesus prove Himself to be your Good Shepherd?

- Jesus modelled what a Good Shepherd should look like, how does this affect the way you lead and nurture those in your care?

- 1 Peter 2:25 describes Jesus as the "shepherd and the guardian of our souls." Take this time to hear His voice and ask Him how He is shepherding you in this season.

Day 05 /
God is Healer.

It has been an exciting journey discovering more of who God is. Today we will get to know Him as our healer.

Isaiah prophesied that the Messiah would come with the mandate to bring about the salvation of our souls and our deliverance from suffering. He said, "But He was wounded for our transgressions, He was bruised for our iniquities; the chastisement for our peace was upon Him, and by His stripes, we are healed." This prophecy was fulfilled by Jesus hundreds of years later. If the prophecy was fulfilled, the promise of what He purchased is ours to claim.

A friend was born with talipes-a birth defect in which the foot is twisted out of shape or position. But Jesus healed her and made her walk. She encountered God as her healer when she was 7 years old. Her hip rotated in its socket, turned 90 degrees to the right, and popped into place.

The word for healed (nir·pā-) in Isaiah 53:5, means to mend and cure. Hearing testimonies and stories like the above or experiencing God's healing in your own personal life can lead us on a quest of discovery. What other parts of us can Jesus heal? How much of us did He pay that hefty price on the cross for? The answer is all of us-body, mind, heart, will, soul, spirit, memory and emotions. He even wants to mend the broken areas of our lives such as relationships.

And it happened when He was in a certain city, that behold, a man who was full ofleprosy saw Jesus; and he fell on his face and implored Him, saying, "Lord, if You are willing, You can make me clean." Then He put out His hand and touched him, saying, "I am willing; be cleansed." Immediately the leprosy left him.

Luke 5:12-13

By His stripes, we are healed! Jesus gets rewarded for the price He paid when we allow Him to bring life into every part of our world; and please note, this life is abundant (John 10:10)! It is not mediocre and not "just enough." Instead, it is overflowing and beyond what we can dream or feel we deserve. His desire for us is to live in wholeness-body, soul and mind!

Jesus gets rewarded, when we allow Him to bring life into every part of our world.

Reflection

- What do you understand about healing?

- Is there any area in your life that needs healing?

- Matt 15:22-29 speaks of the Canaanite woman who was not afraid to ask for healing. Spend some time with Jesus and ask Him for whatever you need in this area.

But He answered and said, "It is written, 'Man shall not live by bread alone, but by every word that proceeds from the mouth of God.'"

Matthew 4.4

LOOKING DEEPER

7

Day 01 / Awareness.

Although most of us know that the Lord is a part of our everyday life, our awareness of Him is a key foundation in living a prophetic lifestyle.

To be aware is "a consciousness of, a sensitivity to, or recognition of." To be conscious of the Lord speaking to us raises our expectancy. We change our behaviour towards looking for what the Lord is saying.

In Judges 6:11, we find Gideon hiding-"Now the Angel of the Lord came and sat under the terebinth tree which was in Ophrah, which belonged to Joash the Abiezrite, while his son Gideon threshed wheat in the winepress, in order to hide it from the Midianites."

Gideon was hiding. He was so focused on what he had to do, consumed with fear of being robbed again. There was no expectancy that the Lord was going to encounter him and send an angel.

We all understand his position right? That feeling of trying so desperately to manage a season of life, overwhelmed by fear; having a full-time job carrying worry and anxiety.

Sometimes we get so focused on what we have to do just to survive that we are completely unaware that the Lord wants to encounter us and lead us to life.

When we are in those seasons, we adapt and use tools we wouldn't normally use. Threshing wheat in a winepress? That has to be difficult!

Becoming aware of His nearness, His relentless love, and His desire to lead us into life in every moment of the day, untangles us from the extraordinary weight of fear and survival.

We train our senses to be so sensitive to the unctions of the Spirit in our daily life that we can go about our Father's business no matter what the external situations are trying to dictate to us. As we train our senses, we become more conscious of the reality of how big He is.

Set your mind on things above, not on things on the earth.

Colossians 3:2

We shift our expectancy from being like Gideon— with none—to knowing that God is moving and speaking to us in any given moment.

Just like Habakkuk says—I will watch for what the Lord is going to say. (Hab 2)

Open your heart and allow your mind to be set on him today. Ask the Lord for a new sense of awareness of His presence.

Reflection

- What are some practical steps you can take that will help you build an increasing awareness of the Lord into your lifestyle?

- What has life been like for you? What have you been most conscious of? Ask the Lord if there is any circumstance of your life that He is wanting to encounter.

- Spend time soaking with the Lord, becoming aware of how close He is and look to Him for what is on His heart to say. Journal your conversation with the Lord.

Day 02 /
Ways He speaks.

Many of us have read the lists of ways God might speak; sometimes those lists can leave us feeling like God doesn't speak to us at all.

It wasn't until I moved to America that I started to understand that God speaks distinctively and uniquely to us. This may sound weird, but I heard His voice my whole life in a Kiwi accent, but when I moved, I could only hear Him in an American accent.

As true as it is that God will speak your language and 'accent,' He will also speak in the way you love to hear things and how He loves to communicate. It might be a faint still small voice, a Scripture, or a child running up and giving you the biggest hug; whatever it looks like, awareness is the first stepping stone. Being conscious of the fact that God will speak to you in a way that is special and unique to you, and accepting and leaning into that, will grow not only your intimacy with Him, but your ability to trust His voice.

He leads us to build a deep unique, intimate relationship with Him.

———

So Gideon said to God, "If You will save Israel by my hand as You have said-look, I shall put a fleece of wool on the threshing floor; if there is dew on the fleece only, and it is dry on all the ground, then I shall know that You will save Israel by my hand, as You have said.

Judges 6:36

I am not sure how I would respond to an angel showing up and telling me I am the one to take on our enemy! However, I would like to draw your attention to the kindness of God. Gideon couldn't believe that He was the one to take on the enemy. Even his response to the angel of the Lord was one filled with all the reasons why he wasn't, yet the Lord showed tremendous kindness.

Gideon was learning of a totally different God. His expectation of God leaving them abandoned was entrenched in his heart and mind. Nevertheless, God took the time to allow Gideon to deal with the insecurities in his heart. Not only was he insecure about what God had said, but he also wasn't confident that the Lord had chosen the right person. He didn't believe in himself.

Through all the ways God speaks to us, it might not be the way we are wanting or expecting. But it leads us to build a deep, unique, intimate relationship with Him.

Reflection

- In what ways does the Lord speak to you?

- Write down one thing that the Lord has shown you in the past week.

- Ask the Lord if there is any new way He would like to talk to you?

- "Sometimes we would rather Him speak in the way we listen rather than for us to listen the way He speaks" (Alyn Jones). Ask the Lord for a fresh revelation on the way He wants to speak to you and allow Him to reveal His heart and love for you today.

Day 03 / Direction.

We can get stuck in the "what's next, what now, where do we go from here, should I do this or that" thought processes. We can go through so many seasons where these questions go unanswered.

Without even realising it, our best intentions are clouded in fear and performance of "not getting it wrong." We can be so consumed with wanting to please the Lord, but finding ourselves stuck. Sometimes, we use fear to guide our footsteps rather than the counsel or direction of the Lord. Fear tells us not to make any move because we need direction from the Lord. Although this isn't necessarily 'wrong,' it is much easier to direct a moving horse than a stationary one.

"A man's heart plans his way, But the Lord directs his steps." | Proverbs 16:9

Trust in the Lord with all your heart,
And lean not on your own understanding;
In all your ways acknowledge Him, And
He shall direct your paths.

Proverbs 3:5-6

These Scriptures show us that it is okay to make plans. Once we have the first and second building blocks, we can take steps forward and know that the Lord will continue to show us the way.

Have you ever looked for a job where it felt like all the doors were slamming in your face, then all of a sudden you received one incredibly perfect job offer or several amazing offers within a short period of time?

Sometimes, everything can just suddenly fall into place. When we plan our ways, God uses everything at His disposal to help enable us to walk in His ways.

In Acts 15-16, we read about Paul's plan to visit and encourage the churches he had planted in the province of Galatia during his first journey. After that, he hoped to take the gospel to unchurched regions. After being redirected twice, Paul was at a standstill in Troas, the Eastern coast of the Aegean Sea. It was there, Paul received the Macedonian Call: "During the night Paul had a vision of a man of Macedonia standing and begging him, 'Come over to Macedonia and help us.'" His companions, Silas and Timothy, had plans to head directly West, but they were "kept by the Holy Spirit from preaching the word in the province of Asia" (Acts 16:6–8).

When we live with the Lord as part of our everyday life and are on the move, we can trust that He will get our attention in any way to help us and guide us along.

Reflection

- Is there any part of your life where you currently feel "stuck?" If so, ask the Lord to show you how understanding Proverbs 16:9 and Proverbs 3:5-6 can bring new insight to your situation. Journal your conversation with the Lord.

- Ask God for a promise or encouragement, specific to your plans and purposes, that you can hold onto in various seasons of your journey.

- Paul received the vision of the man of Macedonia. What does it look like for you when God gets your attention? Spend time with the Lord and ask Him to continue to heighten your awareness of Him so that you can continue to recognise His leading.

Day 04 / Prophetic Dramas.

When our first child was born, he was an amazing sleeper-a dream baby. Until around 9 months old; he suddenly didn't sleep. I was extremely tired and it wasn't until much later that we found out he was allergic to gluten.

One afternoon, a miracle happened! He was in his bed asleep. For all parents of babies, the golden rule is "if baby sleeps, you sleep." I decided to take my chance! I climbed into my bed, closed my eyes, and quickly drifted off to sleep.

I awoke to a sudden, rather loud knock on the door. I quickly got up so they wouldn't keep knocking and wake our son. I answered it and politely told them I wasn't interested in whatever they were selling. I returned to bed and thought "well that's the end of that nap." Without even realising it, I had quickly drifted off to sleep. Again I awoke to a loud knock at the door. This time I was mad! I opened the door and dealt with it, probably rather rudely, I might add. This cycle happened another two times.

On the fourth time, I suddenly became aware that this was not normal. In the space of thirty minutes, I had three deliveries and one sales person knock on my door. I laughed and made an off-the-cuff statement to the Lord, "oh, so is this some kind of prophetic drama or something?"

I heard him so quickly and clearly, "Yes, Sarah, it is. You keep answering the door to worry, stress and other distractions when I have called you to live and abide in my rest." It was an arrow to my heart as He spoke so clearly through my random set of circumstances that had played out that afternoon.

The Bible is full of prophetic dramas; many were played out and pointed directly to the coming of Jesus.

Read Genesis 22-Abraham and Isaac.

There are so many things that point to the coming of Jesus. We are going to look at just a few.

1. Father's intention to give up His only son.

In the same way Abraham was willing to give up his son, we can see how that same intention was in our Father in Heaven. It was a prophetic moment that changed the culture of religion as it declared God's nature. When we read this story in our context, we can't comprehend this action or even what Abraham was feeling at this moment. However, in his culture, so many gods required child sacrifice. Abraham knew deep down that Yahweh was different. He responds to his son and makes this statement: "The Lord Will Provide," simultaneously prophesying the coming of Jesus.

As the story unfolded, we see the expression of our covenant-keeping God. He makes all the effort unconditionally, not dependant upon us keeping up our end. He provided... "For while we were yet still sinners, Christ died for us."

2. Here we see how the ram was caught by his horn—(head) in a thicket.

———

Then Abraham lifted his eyes and looked, and there behind him was a ram caught in a thicket by its horns.

Genesis 22:13

A thicket is a place of thorny plants-this was an amazing picture pointing to the final sacrifice where Jesus was to wear a crown of thorns on his head. He took upon himself the consequences of sin, one of which was poverty. This speaks back to what the Lord said to Adam as he was leaving the garden: Genesis 3:17-18 "Cursed is the ground for your sake; in toil, you shall eat of it all the days of your life. Both thorns and thistles it shall bring forth for you, and you shall eat the herb of the field."

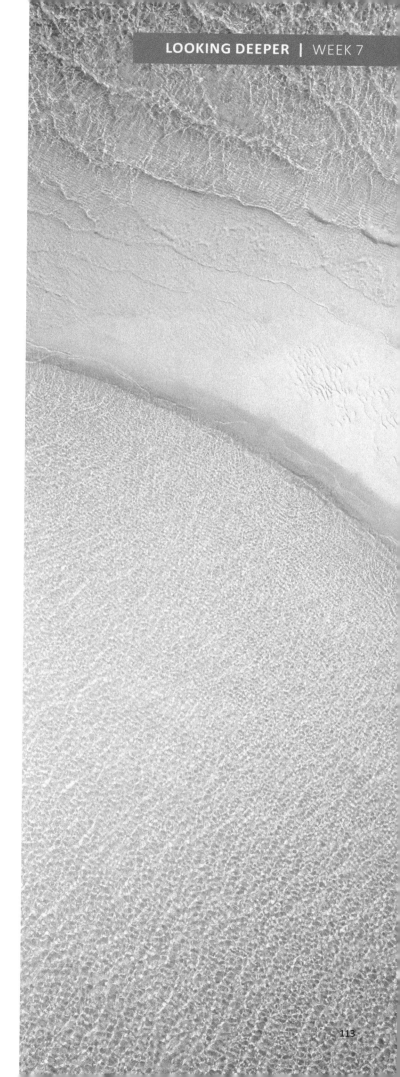

Poverty isn't just a lack of the fruit of our works; it also lives in our mindsets.

"As a man thinks, so is he." | Proverbs 23:7

Here are a couple of other prophetic dramas you can study:

- The book of Ruth-Ruth & Boaz
- Exodus 12-Passover

God can lead you into truth and speak to you in such creative ways. When we live a prophetic lifestyle, a life that is simply connected to His heart and voice, not only is it exciting; it is full of life and love. There is no limit to how He speaks and what He uses to get our attention. Even though we are aware that not everything is a message from God, we live in full expectancy that He wants to speak with us, to us, and through us.

Reflection

- Ask the Lord to highlight a situation that He would like to bring revelation to your heart.

- As you go through your day, look for His heart and voice in the simple things. Journal at the end of your day.

- Look for 'prophetic' dramas in the word and ask the Lord to show you something that you haven't seen before.

Day 05 /
Patterns.

God gets our attention-our heart's attention-when He speaks in specific and unusual ways.

There are so many gems in the Word of God that we can simply miss; however, the written Word is there to be 'mined.' Reading the Word becomes so much more engaging when we understand that it is our delight to uncover the meanings and mysteries that the Lord wants to show us.

One of the many ways God speaks through His word is patterns.

He has left patterns for us to discover and to uncover. His heart's intention in speaking in patterns is often directed at a specific person or circumstance.

Even in a prophetic lifestyle, you will hear of so many personal and unique patterns the Lord uses to get people's attention so they know that He is speaking to them.

The first one we will look at is "verily, verily" which you will find in the gospel of John. Often we just overlook the grammar of something as simple as this, assuming that it is old English. However, he says it twice to ensure our hearts and ears are ready to receive what He is about to say. He is placing emphasis upon the next statement.

He's God-anything He says is as strong and powerful and as true as it gets. His Word is perfect. Once should be enough, right?

There are many occasions where he says their name more than once-we see it with Samuel, Martha, and Peter, to name a few.

Let's look at Peter. The pattern that Jesus uses is so powerful! Peter was the one who has confessed Jesus as the Son of God, then denied Jesus 3 times. Luke 22:54-62 describes the entire denial.

Peter denies Jesus-in front of Jesus-looking at Jesus!

And the Lord turned and looked at Peter. And Peter remembered the saying of the Lord, how He had said to him, 'Before the rooster crows today, you will deny me three times.' And he went out and wept bitterly.

Luke 22:60-62

I can't imagine the depth of shame and pain Peter felt at that moment. There are no words to describe the sheer agony that he would have been in.

However, in Luke 21:15-19, Jesus follows the same pattern of Peter's denial by asking him three questions.

By doing this, He met Peter in his shame and pain and was rewriting a truth upon his heart. He was rewiring their connection as friends and as brothers; moving him from conditional love to unconditional love; moving him out of shame and healing the past. Resetting a new moment in history allowed Peter to move forward from his moment of denial and shame. Jesus was ensuring that he was not bound by his past, but fully free to be what he had called him to be.

In God's kindness, He uses patterns.

God often speaks to us through His patterns—it is the glory of kings to search out these mysteries. He not only wants us to perceive it, but receive it and apply it to our hearts and lives.

For God speaks once, yes twice, yet man perceives it not.

Job 33:14

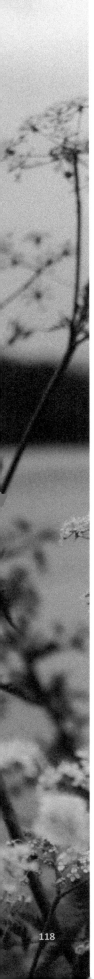

Reflection

As today is the final day of the seven week devotional we are going to reflect over the past seven weeks

- What were the spiritual habits and moments of intimacy that filled you up over the past seven weeks?

- Where is the Lord encouraging you to stretch?

- What is a sustainable daily/weekly/monthly rhythm that integrates the tools you have learnt into your existing times with God?

- How does the Lord want you to continue on your heart/healing journey? What are the key indicators for you to look out for when He is desiring to bring you into a new freedom.

- Ask God to bring to mind a person to send a prophetic word. Ask the Father what He wants to say to them and then write out your word. You can deliver this word via email, voice memo, text message or face to face. Journal with the Lord about your experience.

that the God of our Lord Jesus Christ, the Father of glory, may give to you the spirit of wisdom and revelation in the knowledge of Him,

Ephesians 1:17

Lightning Source UK Ltd.
Milton Keynes UK
UKHW051803090223
416667UK00008B/203

9 780645 311402